Krishawna Crum

THOUGHTS OF YOU

a poetic journey through love, pain,
relationships, & acceptance

For those who feel misunderstood, disregarded, unappreciated.
For those who have lost friends and family.
For those who are single and those who are in relationships.
For those who are waiting for the love they know they deserve.
For all of us who refuse to give up on love, on progress, on life.

Contents

Acknowledgments

I want to thank:

God

My Mom and Dad

My Son Kendarian

My Sisters and Brother

My Family

My Friends (you know who you are)

Every person who has given me advice, encouragement, support, or pain.
It all served a purpose.

Introduction

Thank you so much for taking the time to read this book! I am both honored and excited to share stories about life with you. I believe this book will reveal some of the thoughts, feelings, highs, lows, and everything in-between we experience after a divorce, during singleness, and in relationships. I hope my poems will bring awareness to the feelings both men and women tend not to share with others but, most importantly, feelings that we as individuals tend not to admit to ourselves.

It is my desire that the words herein will provide you with comfort, awareness, and overall peace of mind, knowing that someone has or is currently experiencing a similar situation and/or feeling. I need you to know that you are not alone! Your feelings are valid, your pain matters, and you are not forgotten.

This book was birthed in a season of singleness, but it is for those who are in relationships as well. Perhaps a brief history of myself will shed some light on what gave rise to my poetry.

I am the youngest of eight children and a native of Holly Springs, MS. My dad died on September 23, 1995. His death caused me to feel an abundance of emotions, none of which I knew how to verbally express at such a young age. At this time, I became resentful, never telling my family my true feelings about my dad or my brother. Around age eleven or twelve, I began to journal my feelings. Since I couldn't direct my anger at my dad, I started hating my brother because he was absent. I never had an opportunity to experience a sister-brother relationship, and as a result, I held onto this hate until I graduated from high school. For years, I held this hate because I did not know how to process my dad's death. Because my brother was the closest male in my immediate family, he became the target of my frustration and pain internally.

When my dad died, it took me a long time to understand my feelings toward my brother. It was in college when I finally made sense of my emotions toward my brother and my pain surrounding my dad's death. I learned that I was longing for the love I did not receive from my dad. I became aware that I was trying to understand the unexplainable.

Eventually, I accepted that my brother could not replace my dad. I lost my dad, but I never had my brother. I forgave myself for hating him, and my brother forgave me. I no longer hold any malice in my heart toward my brother. I accept that his path and my path have yet to connect. I may never know what it feels like to have his love, but I allow my heart to remain open just in case the opportunity presents itself.

In addition to my immediate familial issues, I am a divorced, single mother who has been raped. My son is not the result of rape. I conceived my son while married. I have also battled depression in previous years. Revealing this is not easy, but to be in a better place emotionally, I must be at peace with my past and allow what has hurt me to become some form of healing for someone else. I have made an abundance of bad, misinformed, and emotional decisions that have contributed to my frustration, pain, and confusion as well. I am not disclosing pages of my life for sympathy. However, I am revealing my past because I choose not to live life as a victim but instead as an overcomer. Most importantly, I choose to live as a learner of life. Everything that has occurred in my life has helped me to learn and grow. My father's death led me to journal my feelings because it was difficult for me to process them. The divorce eventually led me to seek God more because I lost myself as a result of it. The rape led me to trust God more because I didn't understand how or why it happened. Please understand that pain is a part of life, and living beyond our pain is a decision we must consciously make daily.

As you can see, I do not have a foundation of healthy male relationships—not with my father, brother, cousins, uncles, etc. Yet this book is not about "male bashing" or negative emotions toward men. It is the total opposite: the absence of positive male figures in my family, and life has enabled me to see just how valuable "good" men really are and how we can find purpose and drive in our pain if we choose to always keep going.

Enough about me. Let's discuss the book!

It began long before I knew it would evolve into a book. Some of my poems date back to 2011. However, it was in 2016, after most of them were written, when I realized I had a gift that needed to be shared with the world. So, I hope that when you read these poems, they will speak to your inner being and positively impact your life and the ones you love. This book is not just for single women or women in general. This book is for adults, both male and female, who wish to explore various topics on relationships, love, pain, and acceptance. My writing is classified as "poetry," but I like to call them letters because they were written from my heart to be felt in yours.

Many of my letters were inspired by my own experiences and from those of others. I did not, however, purposely seek out individuals to obtain their life experiences. Instead, I used my imagination, life events, and the direction God gave me to compose my work.

As you read these letters, it is my hope that you find hidden treasures in these words that will allow you to understand your feelings do matter but that they should not dictate your life. I pray that any time you feel lost, confused, hurt, abandoned, or misjudged, at least one of these letters may help you get through life's moments.

Society tells us that our value is determined by something on the outside of us. Please remember that the most valuable part of you is what's on the inside, and some of the most valuable things in life are not tangible: peace, confidence, love, and forgiveness, to name a few.

We were not created to be alone. Therefore, after reading this book, I hope you recognize the value of healthy male and female relationships in *all* contexts because when we work together and appreciate one another, the possibilities are endless. But most of all, our world becomes a better place.

This book comprises four chapters: Apart, Union, Waiting, and Awakening. Every letter is structured in a way that allows you, the reader, to apply it on a personal level. Therefore, the context for most of the letters will depend on the reader's background, beliefs, and life situations. I pray that this book creates a dialogue between parents and children, friends and family, etc. I want these words you read to be the words you feel.

I feel we have become accustomed to not sharing our *true* feelings and thoughts. Somehow, we shy away from sharing our truth, especially painful truth. Freedom comes by way of truth. For this reason, please allow yourself to be free by embracing your truth and choosing to live beyond whatever/whoever has caused you pain.

I share with you these letters so you can share them with others. Whenever you feel alone, depressed, abandoned, forgotten, mistreated, or misunderstood, please remember that you are not alone. It is my hope that these letters prove that. I opened my heart to you so that you can embrace and overcome what is in yours.

Chapter One:

APART

Broken Trust

Where do we go from here?
This point of shock, confusion, pain, frustration...

How do we move?
No, how do we live past this moment?

My mind doesn't know
If I should accept what I am hearing
Or believe what I see
Or make sense of my thoughts.

My mind...

My mind has so many obligations in this moment—
This one moment.

How did we get here?
This exact moment.

How did this happen?
Out of all the things that could happen,
Somehow, this place is where we landed.

I don't know you.
I don't know myself.

I am unsure of everything.

To live this long
And come to a place of not knowing yourself
Seems bizarre.
Very confusing.

Because I knew myself before you.
Well, I thought I knew myself...
At this current time in my life,
My feelings have me in a place
I have never been.

I didn't think you would hurt me this way.
No, not you.
Not the person who was my best friend.
Not the person whom I fought for.

I fought for you.
Emotionally, I fought.

I thought we wanted the same thing.

We did, right?
At some point?

When did you decide to stop fighting?
Why didn't you tell me?

My heart aches...

My eyes hurt...

My mind is tired...

So many thoughts,
Not enough answers.
How do we move forward?

I don't trust you after this.
My heart isn't safe with you.
I have lost a piece of me.

Am I supposed to move on from you
Less than how I came to you?

You took something from me and left me empty.
You stole from me.

You stole my smile,
My trust,
My strength.

I'm left with sadness...

Tears...

Pain...

Weakness...

Is this the person you really are?

Right now, I'm stuck—

My heart...

My eyes...

My ears...

My mind... all stuck.

I'm hurting, and I'm not sure if anyone can help.

I have a scar for life.
Whether or not I decide to move on,
I will not be the same.

Changed forever, yet not destroyed.

I may never be the person I used to be.
But no matter how long or how hard this journey is,
I will not allow the very part of me,
My heart, to become cold.

I won't allow you to tarnish my core.
Yes, you broke something inside of me,
But you did not break me completely.

I will smile again...
Believe again...
Love again...
Even if it's just loving
Only me.

Chaos!

The thoughts are so loud.
Any moment and they can arise.

I get lost in these thoughts...
This noise...
So much that the noise becomes
More real than myself.

The thoughts are so loud.

I'm not this person—am I?

Hard to separate myself from it,
Separate myself from you.

Hard to recognize me apart from you,
Hard to leave all of this behind.

Loud thoughts are just noise,
Unspoken words...
Complete silence.

How can I have so much noise
Intertwined with so much silence?

Chaos!

In my own mind,
In my own heart,
But it's my fight now.

Yes, my fight I'm left to have by myself,
With myself.

But I didn't start this fight alone.
I had help.

I had you—
Well, I thought I had you...

Mistaken...

You were there in the beginning—
Well, I thought it was you.

I don't know who you are now.
The lost you helped to create the lost me.

You left,
Yet I still fight
An internal battle.

How do I win when I am the opponent?

The person I fought for
Is no longer fighting for us.

How can I silence the noise
Without silencing me?

The Idea of You

I should stop choosing you.

What if I am obsessed with the idea of you?
What if you are not real?
What if I want you to be real so bad
That I have made you come to life in my head?
In my heart?

I should stop choosing you.
No matter the time or day,
You appear, and I choose you.
I choose to think of you,
And you are not real.

I have to stop choosing you.
You haven't appeared yet.
You haven't found me.

I have to stop choosing you.
It's not a matter of "should" anymore—
I *must* stop.

I convinced myself that believing in you,
Believing in us,
Helps me to not give up altogether.

But what's worse,
Giving up because I am tired of meeting the wrong people?
Or giving up because I am tired of believing?

Believing is risky.

I have to stop choosing you,
Because you haven't chosen me.

So, today, I give up on us.
Today, I choose myself.

Today, I must believe
That believing in me is enough.

Personal War

My battle is not your battle,
Especially if you created this war.

When I was present,
When I was available,
You decided to check out.

Now that I have decided to stop fighting for us,
You want to fight with me.

You fight for us now
While I fight to move on.

My battle is not your battle.
I didn't want this.
What I wanted was us,
But you wanted you.
Your way,
Your freedom,
Your space,
Your own life apart from me.

My battle is not your battle.
When I was fighting to keep us,
You were fighting to break me.

You wanted me to be okay
With what you wanted.

You wanted me to stop being me
And become who you wanted me to be.

You can't accept who I am,
Because you are not okay with who you are.

My battle is not your battle.
I have to stop fighting to keep you.
It's a battle I'm fighting alone.

I now fight for me,
Because you no longer matter,
And you can sense it.

All of my fighting...gone!

You must fight to find yourself
In hopes of grasping the valuable
Lesson I had to learn:
"Improvement never occurs
When one fights alone."

I'm not fighting for you.
I'm not fighting for us.

My battle is not your battle.
It's now your turn to fight.
Without me.

Lesson Learned

I thought we were worth saving.
I thought we both valued what we had.
Well, at least I thought so.

Was it ever real?

Even for me,
Did I really believe we had the heart of fighters?

Not you—mostly me.
I thought I was a fighter.
I knew what I wanted,
And it was you.

I really wanted you.
But somehow, I let you go.

I did not fight for you at all.

I could have said something,
Written something,
Done something!

I just let you go.

I could have tried something,
Anything.

How could I just let you walk away?

I'm not a fighter.
I'm not sure what I am.

When it was time to decide, I did.

Not sure if it was the best
Or the smartest decision,
But one was made—

One decision
That has become many decisions.

Every life-altering decision
Will reflect the wrong decision I made about you.

I will see you
In all decisions I make.

No matter how much
I want to move on
From this one.
You will be forever included.

I will embrace
Everything and everyone
To ensure I never make the mistake, I made with you.

It did hurt me.
It still hurts sometimes,
But I have become someone way better...
Because of you.

I hurt you,
But I still want to say thank you,
Because who you are helped to make me
Who I currently am.

Doors Closed

To receive more caring words
Than actions from you
Makes you only a talker.

When we grasp onto words,
What exactly are we holding onto?

The energy it takes to believe
Is so powerful and valuable,
So, why waste it on words?
Especially words that are not truthful.

If I'm to believe in you, in us,
I must see
That what you say
Aligns with what you do.

I just have to.
It's a must.

Your behavior,
Your gestures,
Your attitude,
Your consistency...
Those things I can believe.

I know it doesn't happen overnight.
I also know that time will reveal
Whether those behaviors, gestures, attitudes are real,
If they are genuine...

I'm not "less than," sensitive, weak, or crazy.
No, I'm the one who allows individuals
Too much time,
A lot of space,
And plenty of chances
To become the person they say they are.

But those chances have come and gone.
That space is no longer available
For you to take advantage of.

When you did nothing,
I was hoping for something.

A call...
A letter...
Something!

These moments of feeling
Lost, confused, stupid...
I will not visit again.
Not for the same reason,
Not for you!

My time, my mind, my thoughts, my actions
Are too valuable to not be valued.

I have too much to give
To not receive something in return.

Doors are closed,
My ears are not receptive to your words anymore
Because your words have no meaning.

I deserve time.
I deserve thought.
I deserve effort.

Shattered

Tell me the truth and disappoint me,
Or tell me a lie and break me.

I can get over disappointment with time,
But once I'm broken,
Who I am is changed forever.

Every day forward,
I have to discover a part of me
In hopes of becoming whole again.

I now have to learn something
That was so natural to me.

What's scary is
I don't know where to start.

Left out,
Left alone to figure this out.

You said you were protecting me—

Lies of protection,
Love of dishonesty.

It was an illusion.
It wasn't real.

I was living a lie
Because you gave me lies,
And I believed them.

The life I knew no longer exists.

Shattered oh so quickly.
Another scar, another tear.

Different Worlds

My world believes,
Your world doubts.

My world tries,
Your world gives up.

My world is honest,
Your world is denial.

My world hurts,
Your world numbs.

My world frees,
Your world hides.

My world embraces,
Your world runs.

My world cries,
Your world pretends.

My world is open,
Your world is closed.

My world feels better,
Your world looks better.

My world is us,
Your world is you.

Missing Piece

I would settle with visiting you.

To be honest, I wouldn't consider it settling.
Compared to now,
I consider "visiting" a reward.

To see you in my sleep
Would provide such comfort.

I would anticipate meeting you,
Knowing I would have some time with you.

I would have something to look forward to,
Something I could call my own—
My own quality time.

Feeling that you are as real
As you can possibly get.

A dream...

Seeing your face,
Being at peace, if only for a moment.

But it's not peaceful here.
All my senses... buried.

If I feel... it's empty.
If I think... it's confusion.
If I look... it's vacant.

Empty heart,
Confused mind,
Vacant space.
Numb...

You are not here!

You never showed up when I needed you!
When it mattered, you never came!

If I didn't feel this connection,
Then I would be okay,
But I am connected to you.
The thought of you gives me
A sense of security.

I miss something I never had.

Will I ever get it?

I try,
I pray,
I cry.
This feeling never goes away.

My life is not what I wanted.

I didn't create this life without you.
I grew up without you.

How can someone who has never shown up
Be so valuable to me?

Why do you matter?
Why do I care?

I made it.
I made it without you.
I'm still here without you.

This is not a plea for you to show up—
This is really a plea for my heart to let go.

You exist in me,
But I'm not a part of you.

It would be so nice to know
That I am not alone,
That though we have always been apart,
That somewhere,
Someday,
I would find at least a small place
In your heart.

Life's Crossroads

What joy it brings to have you.
Oh, what sorrow it brings to keep you.

I gained so much by losing it all.
I learned so much without knowing enough.

The tears are my reminders,
The smiles are my motivation,
Even if you are not the reason anymore.

The place I was in
Seems to be so foreign,
And at the same time,
The place I'm heading to
Is just as unreal to me.

Going back is not an option.
Staying here isn't, either.

Haunted by memories of pain.
Invited by thoughts of freedom.

Distortion.
Emotionally distorted.

What options do I have?
Do I have any options
On moving from this moment?

Where do I start?
How can I do this?

I can do this, right?

I will argue and fight
To *not* remain here
In this place.

I will.
I have to!

I will move.
I will go forward at whatever rate,
As long as I'm not in this place.
Not here.

I have outgrown that place behind me.
I will eventually outgrow this place I'm in.

Crossroads—
Life's crossroads.

Growing Pains

Just because there is distance doesn't mean there is no love.
What makes growing so difficult to grasp?
What makes us so afraid of growth?

Is it that we do not know
Which direction we will take next?
Or how long will it take for us to get there?

What people may we have to see less of,
Talk less to?

Growing is so much bigger
Than allowing emotions to determine
The value of our relationship.

We may not talk as much now.
We may not see each other as often.
But all the years of being around you,
With you, was for a reason.

Just as not being around you
Serves a purpose as well.

Your growth may be rapid,
Mine may be stagnant
At the current moment.

Either way,
We cannot allow something
So small as distance to diminish how we feel.

We may not have a title
Such as friend, spouse, classmate, or whatever,
But why limit love to a title?

Love is greater than a title.
It goes way beyond categorization.

We may never be able to grow together,
We may even continue to grow further apart,
But no matter the distance,
No matter the reasoning,
No matter what we assume about each other,
The love is still there.

Our love reigns—
Through the pain,
The lies,
The laughs,
The memories,
The tears.

It's through growth that we are at this point.

Let's not think negatively about one another.
Let's embrace our process.

Let's keep growing,
Keep loving,
Title or not,
Close or not.

In Memory Of...

Missing a person I never really got to know...
Nothing outside of me hurts as much
As the pain I carry.

I may never say the truth
But I feel it.

If I returned to that day,
It would be hollow.

Something left when you left.
With my age,
I don't know what it was that left me,
But I know you did.

You left me...

It has been a long time,
But obviously not long enough.

I can cry all day and night...
I'm not sure why.
It comes from the inside.

It's deep...
Unexplainable...

Time doesn't heal wounds,
Because any time you become a thought,
The pain becomes reality.

They talk about you, and I must remain silent.
Silent I have been for a while—

I'm missing the person I never knew.
Does it hurt because I didn't know you,
Or does it hurt because of the things
We didn't do together?

Our time together is almost nonexistent.

I can't remember.
I don't have memories of us.
Just visions of you...
Glimpses of you...

I don't have to visit your grave.
You're buried in me.

If I thought of you daily,
I would cry daily.

Today feels like the first day.
It feels like they just told us the news.

To my face, they said you were gone.
We were there,
But I don't remember saying goodbye.

I don't remember...

I want to remember what you said.
I could ask to see if you said something to me,
About me,
But it wouldn't be the same.

I want to remember hearing you say
That I am beautiful.
That I am special.

Your words...
Your voice...

But I should let that go...
Right?

What's wrong with me?
I'm not eight anymore.

Am I supposed to feel this pain this deep?
Am I still living in the past?

I can choose to ignore
Or to keep covering this dark place,
But maybe that's why every male I can recall
Has never made me feel safe,
Because the man that everyone says was a stand-up guy left me.

People are here, yes,
But I don't think anyone understands
Where I am coming from.

This place...
I know they don't or wouldn't understand this place.

They got more hugs than I did,
They saw you more,
Heard you more.
No, they don't know this place...

I guess that's why I'm different.

I feel different.
I think different.
You made me different.

So I guess I'm used to the silence,
Used to being alone,
Used to being left.

I can get over all of them.
I can get used to a lot.
But the one I can't get over
And can't get used to not being here
Is the one that abandoned me that year.

But that was then,
This is now.

I never said what I had to say,
Never spoke it out loud:
I miss you...

P.S.
Dad, I really hope I am making you proud.

Chapter Two:

UNION

To You...

I stand before
Not this man,
But God.

God, I present my husband to you.
I present this marriage to you.

God these vows are spoken before you,
Because you are the one
That allowed this union.

As I stand before _____,
I know that you answer prayers.

I prayed for a man
I would want my son to learn from.

I prayed for a man
Who was led by You.

I prayed for a man
Who values family,
Who is a go-getter,
Who challenges me,
Who sees me,
Who hears me.

I prayed for so much more,
And now I stand before my answered prayer.

I know this man is not perfect,
But his imperfections are perfectly okay with me.

We do not seek perfection—
We seek *You*.

I know the days ahead
Will not always be easy,
But, God, I also know
That if I was able to make it
Through the years without _____,

Then I know I can make it
Through the years ahead with _____.

I always knew I was created for someone,
That my heart was safe with someone.

So today, God,
I can't thank you enough
For this amazing gift,
But I will start today
By accepting his hand.

Your peace, your love, your guidance
Led us to each other,
And I declare and decree on this day
That your peace, your love, and your guidance
Will lead us to forever.

God, thank you for _____.
And _____, thank you
For agreeing to be God's vessel.
Your obedience brought us here.

_____, I do value you,
I do honor you,
I do believe in you,
In us.

Please remember that I loved you
Before I ever knew you—
I was already yours.

You had me long before we met.
I'm yours _____.
I have always been yours.

Love Song

Before now,
We never knew
Each other existed.

We both have captivating solos.

We perform alone.
Everyone is watching,
Watching you,
Watching me.

Others play their part,
Remaining the audience.

Bright lights beam
On us separately.

Performing,
Acting,
Authentic emotions,
No falsettos.
Everything is pure.

When I release my sound,
They are intrigued.
But for me,
I hear only noise
Because the sound I hear
Is never good enough—
Never enough for me.

Bright lights shine
On each of us individually,
And we do not share stages.

What we share
Is beyond the surface.

Your notes are not like mine,
Yet everyone hears you in me,
Me in you.

Can't remember when
The lights began shining in my direction.
Don't know how long our solos will last.
How long will we satisfy the audience?

This solo requires a lot.
It seems to be bigger
Than what eyes can see.

You shine brightly,
So do I.
But as long as I have cheers
And you have screams,
We will never hear the beauty
Of our notes together.

I don't know you,
But something within
Tells me that you are the only one
Who will perfect my sound.

We can't keep performing
For lights,
For cheers.
We have to want more,
And want it bad enough to let go...

Let go of the spotlight.

Once the lights are off,
The outsiders cease to cheer.

Darkness...
Silence...

Here in the silence
We find the sound
We both have been searching for.

You fit me...

You and I create an angelic sound—
One that no longer involves

Lights or spectators.
The sound alone is enough for both of us.

The moment we discover each other,
We realize we do not need
What we once couldn't let go of.

Our solos are melodies,
And together, we create harmony—
A unique sound composed of endless notes.

We don't require practice,
Nor do we engage in lessons,
Because what's created among us
Is always an original.

Lights dim,
Audience gone,
That moment...
I hear the sound of you.

We longed for each other,
But never knew who.

We were destined...

The moment we took the time
To listen to the song our hearts made,
We found each other's beat...

A love song with the deepest passion...
A song that can only be created
With *you* and *me*.

The Present

You woke me up.
You did it.

You awakened something
I forgot existed.

I was unaware
That I was asleep.

Sleepwalking through life
In hopes of encountering you.

You woke me up.
You did it.

You did it effortlessly.
Nothing grand,
Nothing remarkable—
Well, not to outsiders,
But to me.

Your thoughts are grand,
Your conversations are addictive.

I'm drawn to you.

Effortlessly,
Everything is done effortlessly.

Simplicity—
Simply being you—
Uncovered,
Awakened me.

I can't predict the future,
Won't try to erase the past,
But I'm definitely thankful
For the present:
Your presence.

Love Lost

I forget what it is like to love you.

I walk around as someone
And do not know this person.

I do not know you.

More importantly,
I do not recognize myself.

We lost something
We never had a chance to enjoy.
We lost a part of us.

I see it in your eyes.
I feel the emptiness
When the slightest of your skin
Touches mine.

I want to love you.
I'm here to love you.

You used to enjoy my presence.
You used to be all in.

It's not that I blame you—
I don't.
I just miss my teammate,
My friend.

I'm so lost now.

I'm hurting, too.

Can we hurt together?
Can I wipe your tears
And you wipe mine?

You shut me out,
And you shut yourself out.

You gave up,

And I get it,
But how do we move on from here?

I forget how to love you
Because my love isn't enough anymore.

I don't know if you want my love anymore—
You won't tell me what you need.

Please come back,
Help me save us,
Help me become
The me you met years ago.

I want us back.

Reach for me.
With your eyes, reach for me.
At least let me see you longing.
Let me feel
That you haven't completely let go.

We lost a piece of us
In that cold place,
And in this moment,
I see we died as well.

If we don't try now,
We may never move past this hurt.

I need you.

Help me love you,
No matter where we start.
As long as you are with me
And we try together,
Love can be found again.

I want to remember how to love you.
I want to remember our love.
Will you let me love you again?

Effects of You

He takes me to a place I've never been,
Foreign yet full of bliss.

A perfect place to be me,
But now I don't have to be me
All by myself—
It's now us.

We are the prototype of love.

I never knew it was possible,
But ever since meeting you,
Impossible has vanished.
More and more the unthinkable occurs.

Thanks for being you
And for helping me show
The best of me.

In your presence,
I feel such passion.

Absence from you
Doesn't exist,
Because even when the physical is gone,
My heart will beat your name,
My mind will think your ways,
My soul will sing your song.

Forever we will be,
And that makes this life—
My life—
So much easier.

Love Again

Give your best.
She can take only so much.

Once she's gone,
Nothing you say or do
Will get her back.

Don't lose her.
She's a jewel.
She's like no other,
And you know this.

Don't allow your fear
To rip you from her presence.

She has your best interests in mind.
She didn't ask for the world,
Just your heart.

Your heart is what she is drawn to,
But your heart is not available.

You haven't presented your heart to her.

You are hiding it from her,
Hiding it from yourself.

You allow yourself
To go only so far with her.

It's not past heartbreaks, it's *you*.

You don't believe in yourself.
You don't believe you deserve her.
You don't believe you can be
The man she sees in you.

But you are wrong.
You are wrong about this one.

Don't let her walking out wake you.

Awake the inner you
Before it's too late.

Awake a beating heart,
One that longs for her.

Awake a giving heart,
One that gives to her.

She won't break it.
Instead, she will value the very part
You have been shielding from her.

Her light will help heal your dark places
Because God has prepared her to do so.

Don't let her go.
Take a chance!

Leap.
Leap for her!

It doesn't have to be a big leap,
Just show her you are reaching for her,
Reaching for God.

She will feel your grasping
And will accept your effort.

She will feel the uncovering
Of the place you've been keeping
From her.

She knows.

She feels what you feel.
Just open up.

She's waiting on you
With open arms.

She's strong enough to hold you,
But you are much stronger than you think.

Leaping takes strength.
She sees the strength in you.

She believes in you.

Believe with her.
Be in love with her.

Kiss Me

Kiss me softly, love me always.
Think of me constantly, touch me gently.
Hold me tightly, care for me passionately.
Explore me intimately and do it lastingly.

Kiss me softly, love me always.
Speak to me honestly, look at me deeply.
Listen to me openly, take heed of my words closely.
Criticize me positively and do it sparingly.

Kiss me softly, love me always.
Grow with me continually, reside with me peacefully.
Support me financially, humor me spontaneously.
Surprise me greatly and do so frequently.

Kiss me softly, love me always.
Commit to me daily, trust me willingly.
Smile at me unconsciously, relax me romantically.
Encourage me spiritually and do so genuinely.

Kiss me softly, love me always.
Dream with me creatively, connect with me emotionally.
Pleasure me sexually, want me truthfully.
Age with me gracefully and do so slowly.

These promises, I'm willing to make,
If you promise to always make them with me.

With reminders daily,
I'm ever so willing
Every time you kiss me.

Organic Love

A flower in a drought,
A garden in a desert,
A sweet melody in disbelief,
A hand in a lonely world—
That's what you are to me.

A peace of mind in a world of confusion,
A warm feeling on a sad day,
A comforting spirit in a scary moment—
That's what happens when I see your face.

An addition to my physical being,
Not an addition to my heart.
We were destined to be,
So, there was a place for you from the start.

You allow me to be me,
And I accept your flaws.
I allow you to be the man you are,
And you accept me as the woman I am.

Growing...
We are growing together.

This is organic.
We develop together.

We do not allow our mistakes
To hinder our progress
Because we understand
That love isn't about flawlessness.

Love is about embracing the imperfections
And appreciating the process.

Love alone is not enough
It must be accompanied by many things...
Honesty,
Patience,
Understanding,

Openness,
Just to name a few.

Without these and more,
I can tell you I love you,
But it wouldn't show
In how I handle you.

By knowing this, I allow my actions
To speak to every part of your being,
Even the ones we care not to share.

Growing...
We are growing together.

Don't stop being you,
Don't stop growing with me,
Don't stop sharing with me.

Keep growing,
Keep developing.

Let the love in me
And the love in you
Always intertwine.

Opposite

She's not selfish,
She's not rude,
She's not lazy,
She's not boring,
She's not bitter.
No, not her.

She's giving,
She's thoughtful,
She's hardworking,
She's fun,
She's spiritual.
Yes, that's her.

She's not sad,
She's not irresponsible,
She's not dark,
She's not hurtful,
She's not a taker.
No, not her.

She's happy,
She's responsible,
She's light,
She's helpful,
She's a giver.

Everything she is not, you are.
And everything she is, you are *not*.

Opposites do attract,
But she knows who she is,
Which gives her the strength
To walk away—

Not because it's easy.
It's the opposite.

It's hard for her to receive energy
That's so different
From the energy she's giving.

If it's not who she is,
Don't expect her to take it on
And become who you want her to be
Or who you have been accustomed to.

Because the woman she is
Requires more from you.

Opposite...

Everything she is
Allows her to see it in you.

Her eyes are already opened.
She sees the good in you,
But you can't see beyond your past.

How you handle her
Can't be the same way
You have handled those before her.

No, it must be the opposite...

Different...
It must be different...

Treat her different...
Because she's not them.
She's different from them—
Opposite of them.

Our Journey

If I love you with my mind,
That wouldn't be enough.
I can only do so much.

If I love you with my heart,
That wouldn't be enough either.
I can only give so much.

I can do what I can,
I can say what you want to hear,
But all of it wouldn't be enough.

The only way to ensure our love
Is if we love each other
Through the one that is love.

If I go to God with what
You need from me,
And He leads me,
I can't go wrong.

If you seek God with what
I need from you,
Then it must be right.

Only God can give us what we need,
For us to be all
He created us to be.

The moment we start
To veer away from God
Is the moment we begin
To sabotage what He ordained.

Let's not tarnish this
By leaving out the one
Who brought us together,
But cherish this by inviting
The one who knows us very well.

Please remember,
No matter what I say or do,
Don't alter what God told you.

He has the answers.
He is the guide.

Why would He give me to you
And you to me
If He didn't have the manual on how we work?

We work, sweetie.
God knows we work.

Let us trust God with our hearts,
Leading us every step of the way.

This is our journey.
Let it begin...

My hand in yours,
Your hand in God's,
His hands on both of us.

Safe

I buried my heart,
But when I met you,
I felt something
I had never experienced.

When I met you,
I realized I forgot how to feel...
Feel special,
Feel trusted,
Feel for the opposite sex.

I buried my heart.
After so long, I forgot where it was.
I couldn't find it.
Some days I was glad I lost it.
Other days I wanted it.

I seem to be doing
A lot of forgetting these days.

I forget what it feels like
To be loved by someone
Who looks like you.

I forget how to relax in love.
That it is not me or you,
But the ones before you
That make me second guess.

I forget that you didn't come,
You were sent.

You helped me to remember,
Remember that I do exist
Beyond the physical.

Emotionally, you see me.
You helped me emotionally.

I can go there with you.
There's no limit to us.

Uncalculated depth...
Indescribable substance...

I buried my heart,
Not for it to waste away,
But for it to be found.

I thought I was hiding it from others,
Hiding it from myself,
But now I see I was placing it
In the exact location you would search.

For you...

It was perfectly hidden for you.

After all the breaks my heart endured,
I see it was only broken
To reveal the treasure that was within.

I buried my heart,
But you...
You embrace it.
You cherish it.

Safe...
My heart is finally safe.

Chapter Three:

WAITING

Wanting You

I want your hand on my thigh
And your lips on my neck.

Not just any lips,
Not just any hands,
But the hands of a man
Who longs to hold my heart.

A man who seeks daily
To stimulate my mind,
Not just my body.

I want my head laying on your chest
And my leg wrapped around your leg.

Not just any man,
But a man who has laid
His requests before God,
Making it safe for me
To lay my head on him.

Not just any man
Wrapped up in anything—
No goals, no dreams—
But a man wrapped up
In becoming the man
God created Him to be.

That man is *you*.

I can feel your breath on my skin,
And I'm not on guard about you being so close,
Because you are so close to my Father.

I can see your face,
And I'm not nervous about your presence
Because we don't travel
Where God doesn't go.

I want your hand on my thigh
And your lips on my neck.

This is beyond passion.
This is right.

Yet a part of me has a hard time
Believing you are real.

This is peaceful.
Yet a part of me is not totally at ease.

All my past wrong touches
Have made me timid,
And you sense it with your heart,
But you don't change.
Instead, you touch my fears away.

Your hands touch the places
No one else has come close to.

Every touch from you
Confirms my security.

I'm safe with you.
God made you for this.

You love my heart bruises away,
And I can feel them drifting away
With each encounter.

I want your hand on my thigh
And your lips on my neck.

Your hand is protective,
Strong yet gentle.

Your lips are inviting.
I'm drawn to you from the inside.

I long for your presence.
I await your arrival.

Daydreaming

I can feel you,
But I don't know you.

I'm able to embrace what's not here.
I'm able to believe in what I cannot see.

Your smile brightens my heart.
You're beautiful.

I'm secure with you.
I feel protected,
And you're not even here.

Not visible,
Not tangible,
But your hands were built
To hold my sweetest spots,
My most sensitive areas.

I can go here.
This place created just for me,
For us.

Tears fall,
Eyes close,
And a smile appears
Because of you.

So lovely,
So irresistible,
I can't resist going to this place.

No matter the day or time,
Somehow, I'm able to find your heart.

May these tears water your thoughts,
May this smile gives you peace,
Knowing I'm already yours.

My heart is taken.
My thoughts are, too.
I've placed them with God.
When you are ready,
He will release them to you.

I already love you.
I'm already yours.

Trust it.
It's real.

I can feel it.
I can feel you,
And you're not here.

That's just how amazing you are,
And just how powerful we are together.

Sadly Awakened

When I laid down last night, all was well...
I closed my eyes,
And eventually, I wandered
Into a place of what if.

Searching,
Longing.

In this place, I stumbled upon you.

I saw your smile.
I felt your beauty.

It was real to me.
You were there
In my presence,
In my world.

I laid down last night without you.
All was well.
But when I found you,
Everything became much better.

I saw you.
You were real,
But only for a moment.

The moment wasn't in time—
It was in my head.
You were in my dream.

I dreamed of you,
Of us.

I didn't search for you—
You were already there.

The smile you had was so beautiful.
We didn't do anything special,
Just seeing you showed me
That you are the one I'm missing.

In that moment, my heart was okay
For only but a moment.

It wasn't in this world,
It was in another.

These feelings,
These thoughts,
In a world that's not real.

It ended.
We ended.

I opened my eyes
And saw this world...

Reality.

I woke up.
No us,
Just me.

Nothing I planned,
Nothing I can do.
I woke up with a broken heart,
Because...
I woke up without you.

Resting Place

I keep thinking of your chest—
Not just the physical,
But what lies beneath...

A chest to lay my head on,
But more importantly,
A chest that holds
The heart of a man
Who loves God,
Who loves me.

I keep thinking of your chest.
After a long day,
In the quiet morning.

It doesn't matter the moment.

When I stop and think,
I just want you near me.
To hear you breathing,
To hear the life in you.
That somehow brings me peace.

I just want to feel your skin,
The warmth of your body.
Smell your scent,
The sweetness of you.

I keep thinking of your chest
Because your chest holds
Something valuable,
Something rare,
Something beautiful:
A God-crafted heart...

The place that is wrapped
In power and strength,
But sensitive enough for me
To be at peace.

Your chest...
My resting place.

In-between

Writing to you,
Hoping you hear me.
Don't know your name,
Haven't seen your face,
But at times,
I can feel you near me.

It's amazing how I can smile,
Yet I have never felt your touch
Nor heard your voice.

However, a smile still finds me
Because I believe in you.
I believe in us.

I dream of your smile.
I ponder what makes you happy,
What makes you angry.

I get lost in your sensitivity
And aroused by your masculinity.

I can see my head lying on your shoulder
And you embracing the moment.

You don't push me away
Nor do you pretend to care.
You're genuine.
I'm able to be me without judgments.

Many say you are not real,
And they try to deter my hope.

As much as I want to erase you from within,
It's hard to give up on you,
Give up on us.

I want to say, "Forget it!
Why bother?"
But it's not that easy.

Your existence helps me keep going,
Helps me keep believing.

Yet this waiting
Is really taking a toll on me.
I'm scared...

I'm scared that I'm not whole enough,
That I'm not the person I should be.

I constantly wonder:
Am I ready
For what I long for?

I wish I knew
When you will make yourself known
Because my negative thinking
Happens too often

I haven't met you,
I don't know your name,
I haven't seen your face,
But something so deep within says,
"Keep trusting."

Because what I feel
Is not just a feeling—
It's you.

You have taken hold of my heart,
And even when I have given up,
You remain...
A part of my being,
A part of my thoughts.

So let me go or show up.
Just please choose.
I'm tired of the in-between.

Uncovered

Without you, I'm exposed...
I'm exposed to the elements.

I want to be in our world
Where you and I exist together.

Your plans,
My plans.
Your dreams,
My dreams.
Where only "we" matter, not I.

What is this world I'm in now?

I can't talk to you,
I can't see you,
I can't feel you.
I wonder, do you think of me
When I think of you?
Do you know when I long
For your presence?

Without you, I'm exposed...
I'm exposed to the what-ifs:
What if you never show up?
What if it's too late?
What if all this waiting
Has dwindled the best parts of me?

Without you, I'm exposed...
I'm exposed to time-fillers,
People who take up my time
While I'm waiting for you.

I'm tired of waiting.
Can't you just show up?
Can't you just appear?
When you do show up,
The door closes behind you—
Only the two of us are behind this door.

No more visitors,
No more watchers.

Without you, I'm exposed...
I sit here,
And people can walk by anytime,
Stop by anytime,
And may even stay awhile,
But they are not you.
Only you can make the difference.

I could stop the visitors,
But if I close the door,
I will close you out, too.
I have to remain open
And wait for your arrival.

Without you, I'm exposed...
Don't let everyone see me.
I don't want to be seen anymore,
Not by anyone but you.

Please don't delay any longer—
I'm waiting on you.

Walk through,
And let's live together
In our world.

Show up,
Love me,
Hold me,
Protect me...

Bedtime Thoughts

If I could hold your hands,
I would.
If I could look into your eyes,
I would do that, too.

But since I can't do either,
I'll lie here and savor the moment,
Knowing you exist
Until I can be
With you.

You must be out there
Because this feeling will not subside.
It leaves for a sheer moment
But never really dies.

I'm so curious to know your thoughts
Because I have so many to share.
In due time our season will spring forth,
But in these moments,
Each passing moment,
I wish you were here.

I'm not sad or angry—
I just have so much to give
And no one to share it with.

But our days are coming,
And that is what helps me through.

I smile at the thought:
My blessing,
My friend,
My gift.
Just laying here,
Waiting...
Thinking...
Of you.

Pursuit

Finding you
May be the longest,
Hardest task ever known.

Are you really a person?
Do you really exist?
Or are you some creation I fathom
When my reality doesn't satisfy me?

I'm not really searching
Because if I attempted to,
I wouldn't know where to start looking.

Honestly, I'm waiting for you,
But what if you've stopped searching for me?
How will you find me?

So many questions,
And to simply think of them
Takes a toll on me.

It drains my mental faculties.
To ponder on this at any time
Makes it seem as if something
Is wrong with me.

To come to this place
As often as I do
Doesn't seem logical,
But then I realize
That many of these moments
Are involuntary.

I can keep myself busy,
I can keep myself distracted,
I can become engulfed in something,
Anything...

I can change my focus,
I can change my prayers,

I can even change myself.
But what I can't change
Is you.

Many times, I have constant reminders
That physically, I am alone.
Yet, still without any reminders,
The innermost parts of me arise
And long for you without warning,
Without effort.

I seriously feel
That if this feeling ever goes away,
I wouldn't chase to find it again.

What do I want
That seems so impossible?
Why is it so hard to obtain?
Why do I still care?

Finding you
May be the longest,
Hardest task ever known...
An involuntary pursuit
That I wish will end soon.

Dark Island

Just sitting,
Time passing,
But here (this place)
Seems to be at a standstill.

A world filled with simplicity,
Disguised by complexity...
Excuses, lies, deceit
Infest the good ones.

Everyone's blind.
No fight,
No acceptance.

It's easier to ignore, it seems.
Ignorance creates more chaos in this world.

Just sitting,
Time passing,
But here (this place)
Seems to be at a standstill.

Trapped,
Lost,
Chained to nothing (physically),
Yet I'm unable to move.

It's stronger than me,
Stronger than my will.
My dreams,
My needs,
All seem insignificant.

I have no guidance
On how to get out of this place—
Place of confusion,
Place of no importance,
Place of silence.

No words,
No acts of kindness.
Just here.
A familiar place.

Just me,
Seeing everyone,
Yet no one sees me.

Never Spoken

You are everything I prayed for.
Everything my heart desired.

I am overwhelmed
Because everyone is not as fortunate
To be blessed with such a gift.

I am more than happy
To begin this new journey,
Because this day
Was destined to be.

The Lord knew I needed a friend,
A partner,
A wonderful person altogether.
And that is exactly why
He created you.

I look in your eyes,
And I see happiness.

I look upon your face,
And I see honesty.

I feel your touch,
And I feel loved.

But most importantly,
When I see you, I see my heart.

I felt lost and then I found you.
I was hidden before you came along.

You showed up and gave me true love,
True happiness,
True freedom.

I can't say today
Will begin our future,
Because, as you know,
Our future began

When we first saw each other.

If they say happiness
Makes you live longer,
Then I would have to live forever.

No one has ever made me feel
The feelings I feel with you.

Just the thought of you
Makes my heart smile.

No words in this world
Can truly describe you,
But I can try by saying:
Wonderful,
Gift,
Blessing,
Thoughtful,
Sweet,
Powerful,
Honest,
Strong,
Supportive,
My heart.

So today I give myself to you.

Before God,
I vow to be your support,
Your friend,
Your peaceful place.

Today I vow to be yours
Forever and always,
And whatever follows that,
I am willing to go all the way
If you promise to always go with me.

I'm Waiting

Thinking of your hands,
Not just to feel the touch,
But the love within them.

I can use a hug,
Not just for the embrace,
But for the security I feel
While inside your arms.

We have met before.
Our spirits know each other.
I know you are real.
Just find me.

Thinking of your smile,
Not just to see you happy,
But to see the beautiful soul within.

I can use your presence,
Not just for the company,
But for the comfort I feel
Simply being around you.

We have met before—
I just know we have.

Can't you feel me somehow?
Do you long for me?
Do you ever look?

Please find me.
I'm waiting.
I'm hoping.
I'm trusting.
I'm praying that one day in time
Your eyes will see my tears,
Your hands will feel my fears,
Your ears will hear my sadness,
And your heart will find my heart.

Keep looking.
I'm right here.

Chapter Four:

AWAKENING

Steps

Every day is not a day
In which we take on more;
More on our minds,
More on our bodies,
Our inner being.

Every day we should be releasing,
Releasing all the things
That hinder us from moving forward.

We should be breaking free
From every bad thing:
Bad thoughts,
Bad motives,
Any negative thing
We do not have to accept.
We do not have to accept failure.
We do not have to accept mediocrity.

Just because something is *in* our lives
Doesn't mean we have to take it on.
It shouldn't become a part of you.
Your failures should not be who you are.

Your worries of your child
Should not be what define you or your day.

Your debt should not be
What stops you from having a smile.

Your job should not stop you
From being a loving person.

Your heartbreak should not stop you
From helping someone else.

Chase after your wholeness
The way you chase after your spouse.

Chase after your healing
The way you chase after your money.

Chase after your freedom
The way you chase after the same things that enslave you.
You have what it takes!
We must shake anything
That has become hardened within us,
That prevents us from taking a new step.

If we have to reach down
And use our own strength
To help us to move our own feet,
Then do just that!

If we have to drag all these weights
Until they have no choice but to come off,
Do just that!

When we reach,
God reaches with us.

We can move forward.
We *need* to move forward.

It's vital!

Don't look back.
Don't sit down on your dreams,
Your happiness,
Your wholeness,
Your friends,
Your family.

We can't give up trying to become better.

When we become better,
Everyone we encounter becomes better.

Who said it would be easy?
Why do we think it is supposed to be easy?
What classifies life as easy?
It's life.
It's different for every person.
No one feels the same.
No one loves the same.
No one is the same.

We can't compare
What we see in others
To our own lives,
Because what we see
Is not the whole story.

It's the ups and downs
That make the story beautiful.
Without any downs,
How do we improve?
Grow?
Learn?
How do we learn ourselves?
How do we see our flaws?

It's only when your eyes have been closed
That we appreciate the light.

It's only when we experience pain
That we know what's real—
Real love,
Real friends,
Real living.

We have to believe
And let go of yesterday.

Every day is supposed to be freeing,
An exciting journey with new opportunities,
New blessings waiting...

No matter what the day brings,
If it's a day you are in,
It's a day you can make a difference.
A new day to be a better person
Than you were yesterday.

Let's stop taking on more.
Instead, let us let go of more.

Let go and live!

Every single day,
One step at a time.

Cycles

Just when you think you have nothing,
Nothing to say,
Nothing to give,
Something happens,
Someone appears.

"I don't have anything!

I'm all out of smiles!
I'm all out of kindness!
I'm all out of love!
I have nothing to offer!"

But just when you think you are empty...
Something happens,
Someone appears.

"Why must it be like this?"
When I was full,
I was alone.

Wasted...
Love wasted...
Hope wasted...
I'm all out now.
I have nothing to give.
They took it.
I gave it away.

But just when you think you are empty,
Something happens.
Someone appears.

This...
Why must it be like this?

Life seems to be a cycle.
Which means there is always a chance.

Each time we choose not to give up completely,
We leave just enough room
For the "new" to arrive.

Holding On

These days seem so long
Without you.
How did I get here?
No!
How did I get here?
And you there?

I'm a spectator of this love thing.
I'm watching, but I'm so confused...

When did I lose you?
Where did we get off course?

We ended up in this dead state,
Yet, I am still living?

I loved you so much
I thought we could get through any hurt...
Any disappointment...
Any difficult place...
I just knew we had everything
To overcome anything.

Oh, the phases you go through
After realizing that what you thought and felt
Will never happen.
It's amazing how the maybes and what-ifs keep recurring.

The dreams I had for us...
Gone!
The plans we made together...
Impossible!
The life we had...
Taken away!

Not because I don't believe in second chances—
I do.
But I'm not willing to take a chance
With you anymore.

I have nothing to lose.
At the same time,
I have nothing to give, either.

I loved you so much!
I embraced you!
I was holding you so tight
That I forgot about me.

I diminished myself
Until only a piece of me was valuable...
A very small piece.

I allowed what I was holding
To become so significant
I didn't realize that what I was sacrificing
Held the most value...
ME!

I was the only one that held on tight.
ME!

I dreamed of our dream world...
The plans...
The hopes...
Shattered.
I loved you so much!

I wanted to be everything
You wanted me to be.
So much of me invested
That I couldn't see anything.

Every hope,
Every plan,
Everything blurred,
Tarnished,
Imperfect.
I loved you—
Don't you get it?

Then I realized...
Why didn't I want to let go?
Because I knew I would lose you forever,
And when I lost you...
I knew I would lose myself, too.

Life Scars

We don't fight the same battles,
But we all have some battles to fight.

Some scars are visible:
Black eyes,
Cancer,
Blindness,
Needle marks.

Some scars are beneath the surface:
Betrayal,
Loneliness,
Miscarriage,
Death.

Either way, we are changed forever.
We must recognize that these scars exist.

Yes, they are scars, but not a death sentence.
Our battles have the ability
To reveal some of our greatest qualities:
Perseverance,
Patience,
Hope,
Strength.

There is always room to grow
If we continue to fight.

It's not about winning or losing the battle,
It's about not allowing the battle
To become all we live for.

We can live to fight,
Or we can live to die.

Every day a decision must be made.

Every moment we can fight
To become better,
To feel better,
To live better—
Better parent,
Better friend,
Better spouse,
Better person.

It's a choice.

We must choose to be better,
Choose to not give up,
Choose life,
Choose to fight.

Quitting is easy and looks appealing,
But living as an overcomer
Feels and is so much better.

The mere fact that you made it yesterday
Shows you have what it takes to make it today.

Keep going,
For something beautiful
Awaits your arrival.

Moments

Moments can be small,
On a large scale,
Or neither.

Whatever their length,
They exist to develop us,
To challenge every aspect of us.

Moments can be shared with others.
While sometimes, we encounter them alone.

The people we experience moments with
Can have a great impact on us.
But no matter who we are,
Every moment is experienced differently.

Moments have the capacity
To create many emotions.

It's not the emotions that alter these moments,
But the actions behind our emotions.

Moments can be recurring
Or simply one instance.

It's not the length of our moments
That makes the difference.
What occurs in any moment
Can be life-changing—
Negatively
Or positively so...

We must learn to appreciate each moment,
Embrace each moment.

By not doing so, we miss out on the lesson,
The lesson that's intended to make us better.

Sometimes we stay way too long in something,
With someone,
Doing something.

It's not how we enter our moments,
But how we leave them.

Each passing moment is precious and rare.
Whether spent alone or spent together.

Life itself is simply a series of moments.
It doesn't last forever.

Savior

I met a man today.
He asked me my name.

I just stood there.
I didn't know what to say—

Not because I was unsure
Of the name he was inquiring about.
I was...

I knew the name
And wanted to share it with him,
But I thought about everything
That came with that name...

All the pain,
All the lying lips that spoke it before this man,
All the things I purposely forgot about
That I didn't even want to share with myself.

He asked me my name,
And I froze.
I just looked at him,
And he at me.

He didn't laugh or walk away.
He told me, "It's okay,
I don't need your name,
Just your heart.

It's not what they call you that's important.
I already know who you are."

He told me to take the pressure off
Because this wouldn't be our last encounter.

He told me that when I encounter "new"
To not be so quick to refer to the "old."

While he spoke, I listened.
I didn't feel ashamed or criticized.

He didn't need my name,
What others called me,
What they knew me by.
No, he just needed me—
My attention,
My heart,
My will to try.

I met a man today...
It's only after meeting him
That I realized everyone before...
Never mind,
Not looking back.
I met a man today,
And I'm looking forward.

Forward to all the treasures that lie ahead—
Forgiveness,
Confidence,
Peace.

He spoke to my inner self.
He asked me my name today.
But really,
He asked me for forever.

Forever grateful,
Forever thankful,
For Jesus.

Family

What happened to the gentleman?
Who is gentle toward her?
Who cares about her well-being?
You know the one that loves her...
Where is that guy?

What happened to the gentleman?

Were you not loved enough?
Did you not get everything you needed?
Where did you go?
You do not seem to be anywhere.

How did we get here?
This cold, horrid place.

No matter how long I sit here,
It seems to not be getting better.

Gentle
Man,
Where are you?

When you show up,
Everything changes.

When you smile,
Our world becomes brighter.

When you appear,
Love begins.

Where are you,
The gentleman
Who embraces the tender parts
Of me,
Of us?

Your hands are needed.
Your voice is wanted.
Your presence is valued.

We long for the day of your arrival.
Not sure how, when, or why you left—
Just show up!
We need you to show up!

Waiting for the day,
And waiting it shall be,
No matter how long it takes,
Because you are just that important.

You always have been,
And you always will be.

Gentle
Man,
I am a part of you,
And, as if you didn't know,
You are a part of me.

God,
Man,
Woman,
Child,
Family,
In that order...
The way it was created to be.

Wisdom

Forgotten,
Dismissed,
Silenced...

What is supposed to be a blessing
Seems to be a curse.

During the times when you didn't know
That you needed me,
I've been there.

In your most precious moments,
My presence has been felt.

Somehow, something called time
Has created this distance between us.
Because of the person I am,
You should learn from my mistakes
And grow from my accomplishments.

Forgotten, dismissed, silenced:
Three words that describe me
And everyone that looks like me,
Thinks like me, feels like me.

You forget what I've lost in order for you to have what you have.
You forget that I am the reason you exist.
Without me, *you* wouldn't be here.

I've cried tears so you didn't have to.
Just because you haven't seen them,
Doesn't mean you shouldn't value them.

You dismiss me
When I try to provide guidance for your life.
You dismiss my teachings
About family, relationships, and life.

You dismiss my presence.

Simply having me around
Should be a reminder
That you too can overcome
And become better than me.

Stop and recognize.
Think and embrace.
See and improve.

Expect more of yourselves.
Dream bigger.
Respect more
And love always.

The path you are on has been created
By someone like me.

You haven't arrived here by your own will.
You've received help before you even knew you needed it
And before you came into existence,
So appreciate my perspective
And value my words.

Because not listening
Could make life harder than it has to be
Or maybe destroy your life
Before getting a chance to become me.

Her Mornings

She arose daily to do tasks
That were automatically assigned to her.

Her responsibilities
And her duties...
They all belonged to her.

But before she arose,
She laid there,
Not knowing what the day would bring.

She laid there burdened:
Heart heavy,
Mind wondering,
Body tensed all over...
Because what was awaiting her was
Way bigger than she could handle
And way heavier than she thought she would ever have to carry.

She tried to pray it away
And she tried to pray for it to get better...
Just a little bit.

She yearned for some form of improvement;
The slightest change would have given her hope
Or something to believe in.

But she couldn't lay there long;
She had to arise because of something,
Because someone needed her
Presence,
Love,
Forgiveness,
Time...

But who did *she* need?
Who gave her what *she* needed?
Who was present for *her*
And loved on *her*?
Who?

She arose to her responsibilities
Because that's who she was:
Someone who was reliable and hopeful,
Someone who wanted to give up
Yet still believed.

She sacrificed herself for the sake of others—
Others' opinions,
Others' feelings.

She arose daily with
Pressure,
Weakness,
Insecurities,
Disappointment,
Doubt,
Fear,
Questions—
So many questions...

But she still arose—
One foot in front of the other.

She was fading away day by day
And no one noticed
Because she kept on
Going,
Rising,
Loving,
Forgiving,
Believing.

Confidence

Why is your head down?
Why do you second-guess yourself?
But most importantly,
Why do you allow others
To make you second-guess yourself?

Why is it that you feel
You are not worth more?

Just because you haven't seen it
Doesn't mean it's impossible.

You don't have to be the same to fit.
You fit because you have your own space
Precisely constructed for you.

What makes you special
Is not what you say, do, wear, or believe.
You alone are the reason
For you being special.

There isn't another like you.
Some may look like you,
May dress like you,
But no matter what,
It's only one of you.

You are beautiful—
Inside and out.
If you don't agree,
Maybe you are looking through the eyes
That have been covered
By others' opinions.

Take a moment.

Remove everything that haunts you,
Makes you feel shameful,
Makes you feel inferior,
And, just for once,
Smile at your reflection.

Stand there.

Stand there a little longer.
Embrace yourself
With loving and accepting arms,
No judgments,
Scars and all.

Sweetie, hold your head up.

I can't see your beautiful smile
With your head down.

I can't see the spark in your eyes
With your head down.

Your smile makes your day better,
But, in all honesty,
Your smile makes *my* day better.

Please hold your head up.
We need you.

Stay Here

Your pain is someone else's antidote.
Your mistakes are someone else's road map.
Your voice is someone else's words.

You mattered way before anything happened
Or didn't happen to you.

You matter.

Your life matters.
Your dreams matter.
Your feelings are valid.
It did happen.

Yes, it is painful.
Yes, it is hard.
But just because it's hard
Doesn't mean it's not worth the fight.

Someone else is crying, too.
Someone else is hurting, too.
Someone else wants to give up, too.

What if you keep going
And help them to keep going as well?

What if they see you make it
And believe they can make it as well?

Your pain is someone else's antidote.

Don't hide.
Don't quit.
Don't die.

When you live, I live.

Please...
Stay here.

In the Night

In the night,
She sits alone in the dark.

Just her thoughts, her tears,
And the moonlight—

All alone with these thoughts.
No one knows what's really tearing her apart.

She seems so connected to the one above,
Yet so disconnected from the ones who are close.

In the night, she finds her peace.
She sits by the window and stares upward,
Because she knows God listens to the thoughts,
He sees the tears,
And all the things
That make it difficult to breathe.

She can be so broken.
She can be so lost.
But in this window, she feels whole,
Because she knows she is being seen.

God sees her.
He sees her in the night.

Yes, tears may fall,
Yet mixed with the pain,
Is trust...
She trusts in Him.
She leans into Him.
She stays here with Him.

She comes here to this place.
As she sits in this window, looking up,
All her fears are small,
All her chaos is silenced.
It's just her and the moon.

How can it be so dark,
Yet there is still light?

She rests in one day...
One day, the tears won't fall.
One day, the pain will make sense.

One day...

But tonight,
She will just find a smile
Through it all...
Confused and all,
Hurt and all.

She rests and looks up
Because, even when she feels alone,
Someone is always looking back.

The dark places don't hurt so bad,
Because of the light that shines through.

It provides so much rest.
Yes, in the night.

No matter the time,
No matter the reason,
No matter the circumstance,
She is always able to look up.

Through all the darkness,
There is still hope
In this window,
In all her moments.

The moon always seems to shine through,
She keeps believing,
Keeps praying,
Keeps looking,
Keeps coming to this place
Because the moon doesn't just shine for her.

You see, it also shines for you.

Involuntary Reflex

We go through life,
Then realize one day
That we haven't been living.

Thoughts,
Plans,
Family,
Friends,
Responsibilities,
Children,
School,
Bills,
Spouse,
Goals,
Pain,
Disappointments
All suffocate us...

We go through life,
Then one day,
Hopefully one day,
We realize we haven't been living—
We have been dying.

Dying to be better,
Dying to have more,
Dying to move forward,
Dying to overcome,
Dying to prove others wrong,
Dying to be seen,
Dying to be heard.

We have been suffocating ourselves.
We go through life suffocating!

We become so engulfed
In trying to live life
That we fail to realize
That life doesn't come,

Life *is*...

We strive to live
As if it's something we must go after.

Life is a gift,
And we should receive it,
Accept it,
Embrace it.

We go through life suffocating,
Then one day, we realize
That we must make the involuntary
Voluntary.

Breathe...

Breathe on purpose...

Inhale the sweetness of life...
Release the tensions of the world...
Your world.

Breathe...

Your family needs you to breathe.
Your children need you to breathe.
This Earth needs you to breathe.

Inhale the great things you see,
The great things you've done.

You deserve to breathe.
You deserve to live.
That's why you are here.

Take a moment...

Many moments...
Daily
To listen to you,
Notice you,
Love on you.

Let go...

You have too much in your hands
That shouldn't be carried by you.

Your hands can only hold so much.
Your heart can only take so much.
Your mind can only think so much.
Daily...
Stop.
Don't carry.
Don't think.
Don't feel.
Just breathe.

The life is not outside of you—
The life is within you.

Beautifully Broken

It's not that I let you go—
You pushed me away.

It's not what I wanted to do—
You made the decision for both of us.

I thought about you
And all the what-ifs.

I thought it was me.
It had to be *me*.
I was so convinced it was me
That I was willing to look
Beyond all the pain,
Beyond all the tears
To continue something that barely started.

I believed in us.
I believed we could make it,
But the decision was made,
And I became numb,
Not letting life be lived.

I became silent.
I became invisible.

No one sees my tears.
No one hears my heart breaking.
No one feels my pain.

I walk around with the pain,
The guilt,
The frustration.
You think this is freedom—
This is prison
Because the world doesn't see the real you.

Not the you you're comfortable with,
Not the you everyone is expecting,
But the you before the pain.

Oh, if you only knew the real you.

You can't lose yourself
If you never discovered who you are.
You must reveal yourself to yourself.

Look beyond the now.
Try it.
Try seeing yourself as God sees you.

See yourself as the person who dreamed
When there wasn't a reason to dream.

The world needs you.
I need you.
Someone you haven't met needs you.

Remove the weights,
Remove the lies,
The cheating,
The divorce,
The breakup.
Remove the jail sentence,
The prison sentence,
The rape,
The drugs,
The alcohol.

Remove those "you're not good enough" thoughts,
Those "no one loves me" thoughts.

Remove the death of your father,
Your mother,
The sick child,
The family you didn't get.

Remove the "almost was" and "almost did."
Remove the food addiction,
The illness,
The "why me" thoughts.

Remove the fear,
The anxiety,
The anger,
The disappointment,
The pretending.

Reveal the truth—
The true you.
You are beautiful.
You are valuable.

There is only one you.

Don't give anyone the power to stop you
From reaching all the treasures on your path.

Don't stop.
Don't stop believing.
Don't stop dreaming.
Don't stop trying.

If you must crawl, do it!
If you have to take a rest stop, do it!
If you have to ask for a helping hand, do it!

This is your path.
Own it.
You are worth it.

Fight for you.

God believes in you.
He has given you all you need
To push through.

You are not flawed—
You are different.

You are not lost—
You are finding yourself.

You are not "less than"—
You are discovering more.

Trust God.
Trust the process.

You were not sent here
To get everything right.

Take the pressure off,
One day at a time.

Embrace each moment.
You do matter.
Your story is worth the journey.

You have what it takes!

Take something so ugly,
So painful,
So devastating,
So hard—
Make it *beautiful!*

P.S. If you ever feel alone,
Remember, you always have me.

Love,
The person who is reading this.

Not Forgotten

I thought of you today.
Don't give up.
Keep trying.
With every try
Comes more experience.

You're learning
In the process...
You are learning something,
Gaining something.

I thought of you today.
It's not too late.
If you are reading this,
Then it's perfect timing.

You have a supporter.
I believe in you.

The strength is not given in total—
The strength is obtained in each step you take.

If you are not taking any steps,
Sweetie, you will never see the amazing strength,
The inexplicable strength
Within you.

I thought of you today.
Yes, you are in this place.
No, you can't change the past.
Yes, you want to do it all over again,
But you can't.

The hurt you feel shows growth.
It shows you are not the person you thought you were.
It means you see the hurt you caused,
And by seeing the hurt,
You now can become a better person,
Ensuring that you do not cause the same hurt anymore.

Lives change.

People live.
People die.
People grow.
You have grown.
Your eyes have been opened.

You are not forgotten.
You are in there,
But someone out here
Is thinking of you,
Praying for you.

Change the world
By helping to change those in your world.

You matter,
And I do not know you.
Imagine how you matter
To those who do know you.

You matter,
And you can still make a difference.
Your location doesn't determine your value—
You were born valuable.

I thought of you today.

Your today looks like your yesterday.
Everything seems to pull on you.
Nothing or no one seems to invest in you.
You are just giving
Your time,
Your body,
Your money.

You are not alone.
The strength to live the life you live
Is inspirational.

You inspire me.

You live selflessly
When you want to be selfish.
You push others to be better,
Yet no one pushes you
How do you do that?

Superpowers.

Superwoman—
Everything you touch
Multiplies.

Superman,
Your presence alone
Changes the atmosphere.

About the Author

Krishawna Crum was born and raised in Holly Springs, Mississippi. She graduated from the University of Mississippi. She currently works in the healthcare field.

In addition to her day job and being a mother, Krishawna has written *Thoughts of You: A Poetic Journey through Love, Pain, Relationships, and Acceptance*. This is Krishawna's first work and is a collection of thought-provoking poetry that touches on many life experiences and what Krishawna herself has managed to survive.

She also devotes her time to helping others and believes in giving to those who are in need. Krishawna hopes that her writing will provide some inspiration for others and help them grow from their life experiences, rather than being defined by them.

Special Note from the Author

Thank you for taking a journey through life's pages. I hope you come along and experience our next journey together because more is in store.

In the meantime, you can connect and follow me at:

- Email: krishawnatheauthor@gmail.com
- Facebook: www.facebook.com/krishawna.crum
- Instagram: https://www.instagram.com/ms_krishawna/
- Website: www.krishawnatheauthor.com

Anytime you stumble along your journey, I hope you can refer to something within this book that will help you to not give up. Remember, your journey is not like anyone else's, so embrace your uniqueness. Please give the world what it is missing, the authentic YOU. *One* page of your story doesn't have to be your *life's* story. You can rewrite it, just turn the page.

Love,